SE   '10

W9-AAY-487

Put Beginning Readers on the Right Track with ALL ABOARD READING™

The All Aboard Reading series is especially designed for beginning readers. Written by noted authors and illustrated in full color, these are books that children really want to read—books to excite their imagination, expand their interests, make them laugh, and support their feelings. With fiction and nonfiction stories that are high interest and curriculum-related, All Aboard Reading books offer something for every young reader. And with four different reading levels, the All Aboard Reading series lets you choose which books are most appropriate for your children and their growing abilities.

Picture Readers

Picture Readers have super-simple texts, with many nouns appearing as rebus pictures. At the end of each book are 24 flash cards—on one side is a rebus picture; on the other side is the written-out word.

Station Stop 1

Station Stop 1 books are best for children who have just begun to read. Simple words and big type make these early reading experiences more comfortable. Picture clues help children to figure out the words on the page. Lots of repetition throughout the text helps children to predict the next word or phrase—an essential step in developing word recognition.

Station Stop 2

Station Stop 2 books are written specifically for children who are reading with help. Short sentences make it easier for early readers to understand what they are reading. Simple plots and simple dialogue help children with reading comprehension.

Station Stop 3

Station Stop 3 books are perfect for children who are reading alone. With longer text and harder words, these books appeal to children who have mastered basic reading skills. More complex stories captivate children who are ready for more challenging books.

In addition to All Aboard Reading books, look for All Aboard Math Readers™ (fiction stories that teach math concepts children are learning in school); All Aboard Science Readers™ (nonfiction books that explore the most fascinating science topics in age-appropriate language); All Aboard Poetry Readers™ (funny, rhyming poems for readers of all levels); and All Aboard Mystery Readers™ (puzzling tales where children piece together evidence with the characters).

All Aboard for happy reading!

Wauconda Area Library
801 N. Main Street
Wauconda, IL 60084

To L.
-SF

GROSSET & DUNLAP
Published by the Penguin Group
Penguin Group (USA) Inc., 375 Hudson Street, New York, New York 10014, U.S.A.
Penguin Group (Canada), 90 Eglinton Avenue East, Suite 700, Toronto, Ontario, Canada M4P 2Y3
(a division of Pearson Penguin Canada Inc.)
Penguin Books Ltd, 80 Strand, London WC2R 0RL, England
Penguin Ireland, 25 St Stephen's Green, Dublin 2, Ireland (a division of Penguin Books Ltd)
Penguin Group (Australia), 250 Camberwell Road, Camberwell, Victoria 3124, Australia
(a division of Pearson Australia Group Pty Ltd)
Penguin Books India Pvt Ltd, 11 Community Centre, Panchsheel Park, New Delhi—110 017, India
Penguin Group (NZ), Cnr Airborne and Rosedale Roads, Albany,
Auckland 1310, New Zealand (a division of Pearson New Zealand Ltd)
Penguin Books (South Africa) (Pty) Ltd, 24 Sturdee Avenue,
Rosebank, Johannesburg 2196, South Africa

Penguin Books Ltd, Registered Offices: 80 Strand, London WC2R 0RL, England

The scanning, uploading, and distribution of this book via the Internet or via any other means
without the permission of the publisher is illegal and punishable by law. Please purchase only
authorized electronic editions, and do not participate in or encourage electronic piracy of
copyrighted materials. Your support of the author's rights is appreciated.

Photo credits: cover/title page: © Harry How/Getty Images; page 4: © Damian Strohmeyer/
Sports Illustrated/Getty Images; page 6: © Bob Martin/Sports Illustrated/Getty Images;
page 9: © Dave Sandford/Getty Images; page 11: © Bill Smith/NHLI via Getty Images;
page 12: © Bill Smith/NHLI via Getty Images; page 14: © Bill Smith/NHLI via Getty Images;
page 16: © Thom Kendall/Getty Images; page 18: © Harry How/Getty Images;
page 20: © Jamie Sabau/NHLI via Getty Images; page 21: © Harry How/Getty Images;
page 24: © Jeff Vinnick/Getty Images; page 25: © Mitchell Layton/Getty Images;
page 28: © Scott Cunningham/NHLI via Getty Images; page 30: © Darren Carroll/Sports
Illustrated/Getty Images; page 35: © AP Photo/Tobin Grimshaw; page 37: © Justin K. Aller/
Getty Images; page 39: © Bruce Bennett/Getty Images; page 40: © Lou Capozzola/Sports
Illustrated/Getty Images; page 42: © Bruce Bennett/Getty Images; page 46: © Harry How/
Getty Images; page 48: © David E. Klutho/Sports Illustrated/Getty Images.

Text copyright © 2010 by Penguin Group (USA) Inc. All rights reserved.
Published by Grosset & Dunlap, a division of Penguin Young Readers Group, 345 Hudson Street,
New York, New York 10014. ALL ABOARD READING and GROSSET & DUNLAP
are trademarks of Penguin Group (USA) Inc. Printed in the U.S.A.

Library of Congress Control Number: 2010015711

ISBN 978-0-448-45447-4   10 9 8 7 6 5 4 3 2 1

ALL ABOARD READING™

Station Stop 3

HOCKEY HOTSHOTS
YOUNG STARS OF THE NHL

by Steele Filipek
with photographs

Grosset & Dunlap
An Imprint of Penguin Group (USA) Inc.

Wauconda Area Library
801 N. Main Street
Wauconda, IL 60084

USA! USA!

It's New Year's Day 2010, and the people in the stands at Fenway Park in Boston, Massachusetts, are cheering like crazy. But the fans aren't cheering for their baseball team, the Red Sox. They're cheering for their hometown hockey team, the Boston

The 2010 Winter Classic

Bruins, who just beat the Philadelphia Flyers 2–1 in the NHL Winter Classic!

The Winter Classic, which started in the 2007–2008 season, has become one of the biggest games of the year for the National Hockey League (NHL). Over 32,000 fans pack the stands to watch a hockey game on an ice rink built on top of a baseball field. But there was more excitement in store for the fans this year in Boston.

At the end of this Winter Classic, the United States Olympic Committee was going to announce the members of the US Olympic Hockey Team. The 2010 Winter Olympics in Vancouver, Canada, were only six weeks away. American players and fans had been waiting months for this moment.

The committee wanted to pick the best players for the job. They knew the US team would face a lot of tough opponents. Alexander Ovechkin, the NHL's leading scorer for two straight years, had already been named to the Russian team. Sidney Crosby, captain of the Pittsburgh Penguins, was on Team Canada.

One by one, the names for the US team are announced: Dustin Brown, Ryan Callahan, Chris Drury. These are young guns—quick hockey players with blistering slap shots! Then the youngest hockey hotshot of them all is named to the team: 21-year-old Patrick Kane!

Three cheers for Team USA!

The second-to-last name that is announced surprises almost everybody. Jonathan Quick, one of the youngest starting goalies in the league, is named to the Olympic team.

After the announcement is finished, the fans go wild in the stands. This is their US hockey team! They are a good squad, but it won't be easy for the US to take home the gold. Jonathan Quick, just 23 years old at the time, has only been playing in the league for two seasons. Patrick Kane, only 21, is the youngest player on the roster. The two have played against each other several times in the regular season, but they'll have to unite to help defeat Sidney Crosby, Alexander Ovechkin, and the other young hotshots of hockey at the Olympics.

PATRICK KANE

Patrick Kane grew up in Buffalo, New York, and showed a lot of promise in hockey from a young age. At the age of four, his father, Patrick Sr., would take him to watch their hometown hockey team, the Buffalo Sabres. But Patrick seemed to be studying the players and their moves, not watching the mascot like most other kids that age! By seven, Patrick was playing organized hockey. He was a natural right from the start.Within six years, Kane was known as one of the top young hockey players in the state. He sometimes played up to 300 games a year and practiced twice a day. Parents of the older kids he played against even complained that Patrick scored too many goals!

When Patrick was 14, he was spotted by former NHL player Pat Verbeek during a tournament. Verbeek was so impressed with Patrick's skills that he asked Patrick to move to Detroit, Michigan, with his parents and play for his AAA hockey club, Honeybaked. It was a huge honor. Honeybaked AAA was one of the top amateur teams in the country and had produced over a dozen NHL players!

Patrick (second from left) poses with two NHL stars—and former London Knights players!

Patrick and his parents thought the opportunity was too good to pass up. The Kane family moved to Detroit, and Patrick began playing against some of the best young hockey players in the nation. Patrick was a superstar who stood out among all the competition. So it was no surprise when he was drafted three years later by a different amateur team, the London Knights of the prestigious Ontario Hockey League. After he scored 145 points in his first year with the Knights, Patrick was awarded the Emms Family Award for rookie of the year in the Ontario Hockey League.

Pretty soon, scouts began mentioning Patrick Kane as a solid choice for the first overall pick in the 2007 NHL Entry Draft. That year, the Chicago Blackhawks had the first pick in the draft.

Chicago is one of the oldest teams in

the league but hasn't won a Stanley Cup since 1961. By 2007, they had been one of the worst teams in the league for almost 10 years. Attendance at their games was at an all-time low. The Blackhawks needed a major superstar to help them win games and bring in fans.

The Blackhawks thought Kane was just the kind of player they needed. They chose Patrick as their first pick in the draft and signed him to a three-year deal. He was going to be their starting right winger—a forward

Patrick celebrates a goal with his teammates.

In uniform for the Blackhawks

who relied on speed and crisp passes to pick up loose pucks and score goals—and he was only 18 years old!

Patrick didn't disappoint his fans. In his first season, he scored 21 goals and 72 points (points are the combined number of goals and assists), which was good enough to win him the Calder Trophy for rookie of the year.

In his second season, Kane again scored over 70 points and was named to the NHL All-Star team. More importantly, he led Chicago to the play-offs for the first time since 2002! The team took down the Vancouver Canucks and Calgary Flames in the first and second rounds of the playoffs, where Patrick scored nine goals. The Stanley Cup Finals were only one series away. But one thing stood in their way: the Detroit Red Wings.

The Red Wings are one of the Blackhawks' oldest rivals. The Red Wings had won the Stanley Cup just a year before, beating the Pittsburgh Penguins, and had won three others since 1997. Kane played well in the series, but the Blackhawks were completely overpowered in five games by the much stronger and more experienced Red Wings team.

The Blackhawks got their chance at Stanley Cup glory the following year, though. Kane took his team all the way to the 2009–2010 Stanley Cup Finals against the Philadelphia Flyers. Both teams fought hard, but in the end the Hawks took the Cup back to Chicago, thanks to a game-winning overtime goal by Patrick! Chicago's young superstar had pulled through, showing grace and poise under pressure. Blackhawks fans everywhere rejoiced; Patrick had won Chicago its first championship since 1961!

The Blackhawks win the Stanley Cup!

JONATHAN QUICK

For most of his life, Jonathan Quick knew he wanted to be an NHL goalie—but he also knew it wouldn't be easy. Goalies have to face slap shots and help set up defensive plays by passing the puck, all while keeping calm under pressure.

But that's what Quick wanted, and he wanted it more than anything. After transferring from his hometown school of Hamden High at the age of 16 to the prestigious Avon Old Farms Prep in Connecticut, he showed the hockey world what he was made of. Quick led Avon to two straight New England Prep Championships in 2004 and 2005. In his final two seasons in high school, Quick himself only lost three games total! In his senior year alone, he won 25 games and posted nine shutouts. Thanks to his quick hands and graceful movement around the goal crease, Jonathan Quick stood out among American goalie prospects.

After high school, Quick moved to Amherst, Massachusetts, to attend college and play hockey. But Quick struggled in his first season, leading the University of Massachusetts Minutemen to a 13-23-2 record. But he focused on his game during

Quick in net for UMass

the off-season and won 19 games the next year. He also significantly dropped his goals-against-average (the number of goals opponents scored against him). Partly because of this, UMass won a place in the NCAA tournament for the first time ever!

Despite a stellar high school and college career, Quick wasn't selected until the third round of the 2007 NHL Entry Draft by The Los Angeles Kings. The Kings weren't entirely sure that Quick had what it takes to be an NHL goalie. Jonathan knew he would have to prove himself there. Like most rookies, Quick started out playing for one of the Kings' minor league teams. In his first season, he suited up for the Reading Royals, the Kings' minor league team for their most inexperienced players. Jonathan had a great season with the Royals and won 23 games. After that, he was brought up to the Manchester Monarchs, the Kings' top minor league team, which was just one step away from the NHL. He was just as good there, leading his team to the play-offs!

Shortly after, Quick got his big break. The Kings temporarily needed an extra goalie for their NHL team. So on December 6, 2007, Jonathan Quick suited up for his first NHL game, and helped the Kings beat the Buffalo Sabres, 8–2!

Quick found a long-term home with the

Kings shortly after that. The Kings' starting goalie, Erik Ersberg, was seriously injured in the middle of the 2008–2009 season. Los Angeles decided to bring Quick up to the NHL for an extended stay.

Some fans worried that Quick wasn't ready for the pros. Many top prospects are unable to handle the speed of the professional game, no matter how good they are in the minors. Even Quick was shaky in his first two games. In his first, he let in a goal on just eight shots and played for only 17 minutes. In his second, Quick allowed five goals against the Detroit Red Wings.

But in his third full game of the season, Quick posted a shutout (meaning no one scored a goal against him) over the Columbus Blue Jackets. Saving all 24 shots, he showed the speed and positioning that had gotten him to the top of the minor leagues. He would go on to win 20 more games that season. Although the Kings finished in last place that season, Jonathan Quick had secured his spot as the team's starting goalie.

Quick remained focused in the off-season, and, in 2009, led the Kings to their hottest start in a decade! The Kings even went on to make the play-offs that season, thanks in part to Quick's amazing plays.

Quick makes a save during his 3–0 shutout of the Columbus Blue Jackets.

In just his third season in the NHL, the young goalie had taken the Kings from one of the worst teams in the league to a serious play-off contender! With his whole career ahead of him, it's only a matter of time before Jonathan takes them even further: the Stanley Cup.

ALEXANDER OVECHKIN

Even when he was just a kid growing up in the USSR (which is now Russia), Alexander Ovechkin knew he wanted to be a hockey player. In fact, once when he was in a toy store with his parents, young Alex grabbed a toy hockey stick and refused to let go!

Sports were a big part of life in the Ovechkin family. Alex's father, Mikhail, was a soccer player. His mother, Tatyana, was a basketball star who had won gold medals at the 1976 and 1980 Olympics for the USSR team. Alex's brother, Sergei, who was 15 years older than him, was already an up-and-coming hockey star. Sergei even taught Alexander how to skate when he was just three years old! In a family like that, it's no wonder that Alexander was interested in sports.

But life wasn't all fun and games for young Alex. In 1995, tragedy struck the Ovechkin family. Sergei, who was just 25 years old, died in a car accident. Ten-year-old Alex took his brother's death very hard. To this day, he still refuses to talk about the accident. But at the time, it was the spark that young Alex needed to continue playing hockey. Hockey was Sergei's favorite sport, and Alex wanted to play on in his memory.

In 2001, at just 16 years old, Alexander was recruited by Dynamo Moscow. Dynamo Moscow is one of the oldest professional hockey teams in Russia. Competition on this prestigious team is tough, and Alexander was one of the youngest players. Most players were over 20 years old and much more experienced, so Ovechkin scored only four points—two goals and two assists—in 22 games in his first year.

Alex didn't give up, though. He continued to work hard, and by his third season in 2003–2004, he had scored over 50 points and was known across Russia as one of the country's top young players. The Florida Panthers of the NHL tried to draft him early, in 2003, but the NHL wouldn't allow it due to Alexander's

age. He was just 17, and the NHL required players to be 18 before the start of the season.

Alex got his big chance the following year, though. The Washington Capitals had the first pick in

Alex in uniform for Team Russia

the 2004 draft. The team decided to bet on Alex, and chose him first.

In 2005, Ovechkin signed a contract with the Caps that was worth nearly one million dollars per season. As a left winger—a forward who would have to play just as much defense as offense—he would be one of the most important and visible players on the ice. He was up for the challenge, though. Finally, Alexander would have his chance

to shine on hockey's brightest stage.

Alex trained hard in the off-season, and in his rookie season of 2005–2006, Ovechkin outscored another young hockey star, the Pittsburgh Penguins'

Alex poses with his brand-new Caps jersey!

Sidney Crosby, with 106 points. That was the third-most points in the league! Even though Alexander was still getting used to the league and its style of play, he was already considered one of the best players in the NHL.

But in Ovechkin's second season, in 2006–2007, the Capitals missed the play-offs again, while Sidney Crosby led the Pittsburgh Penguins to a play-off spot. Not only that, but Ovechkin scored only 92 points, far fewer than his rival, Crosby. People began to wonder: Would Alexander live up to his potential? Would he ever be able to lead the Capitals to the post-season?

But Alexander didn't listen to his critics. In 2007–2008, he made it his priority to get the Capitals into the post-season. Aided by Russian legend Sergei Fedorov, Ovechkin led the Capitals on a late season push to win first place in the Southeast Division! Plus, he scored 65 goals. That was more than any player had scored since former hockey great Mario Lemieux, almost 10 years before.

Though the Capitals lost in the first round of the play-offs to the Philadelphia Flyers, Alexander had a banner year. He won the Hart Memorial Trophy as the league's most valuable player (MVP), the Maurice Richard Trophy for most goals (65), and the Art Ross Trophy for most points (112). Most importantly, though, Ovechkin was voted by the rest of the players in the NHL as the most outstanding hockey player, earning him the Lester B. Pearson Award. Almost every player to win this award has been inducted into the Hockey Hall of Fame. It was clear to hockey fans all over that Alexander Ovechkin had a bright career ahead of him.

SIDNEY CROSBY

A lot of people argue about who is the best young player in hockey. Washington Capitals fans will definitely say Alexander Ovechkin. Patrick Kane is a big favorite in Chicago. Goalie fans say it's Jonathan Quick. But only one young hockey hotshot was named captain of his team: Sidney Crosby.

Growing up in Nova Scotia, Canada, there wasn't much for Sid to do *except* play hockey. By the time Sidney was three, he could skate. By seven, just after he'd begun to play hockey in organized leagues, he had given his first interview. He'd even nearly destroyed his parents' dryer by constantly shooting hockey pucks at it. Nothing could stop Sidney from playing the sport he loved.

It was hard for the Crosby family, though. Sidney's parents didn't have a lot of money, so they made sacrifices to keep Sidney playing. They sometimes cut back on groceries. Once or twice, they missed mortgage payments on their house. But more than anything else, the Crosbys wanted Sidney to fulfill his dream of playing in the NHL. So Sidney kept playing. And as he practiced and played, he earned a lot of attention for his skill—especially after he scored 72 goals in just 57 games for Shattuck-St. Mary's Prep School. It became difficult to keep the media under control, even at Sidney's young age!

Sidney had only played one year of Midget AAA hockey before he was drafted by Rimouski Océanic of the Quebec Major Junior Hockey League (QMJHL) in 2003. An amateur league of young (junior) hockey players, the "Q" has had dozens of future pros play for its teams.

Crosby in action for Rimouski Océanic

If Crosby was intimidated, though, he didn't show it. In Sidney's first exhibition game with Rimouski Océanic, he scored eight points. By season's end, he had scored 54 goals in 59 games and was named the QMJHL's rookie of the year. He won five other trophies that year, including league MVP!

Because of his stellar playing, Sidney was named to the Canadian World Junior Championship team in 2004. Facing off against superstars from the United States, Russia, and other nations from around the world, Sidney was just one of the many famous hockey hotshots playing for a chance to win gold. Sidney and Team Canada eventually lost to the US 4–3 in the gold-medal game. Sidney realized he had to work even harder if he wanted to compete with the world's best young superstars. Silver was okay, but Sidney had his eye on the gold.

In the 2005 tournament, Sidney scored nine points and took Canada to the title game to face off against Russia . . . and a young hockey player named Alexander Ovechkin! Crosby didn't score any goals, but he did help guide his team to a 6–1 win. It was Canada's first junior championship gold since 1997!

After that success, Crosby was ready to bring his career as an amateur hockey player to a close and take the step to pro. Sidney officially entered the 2005 draft with only one question on his mind: Which team was he going to lead to the Stanley Cup?

THE HUNT FOR THE STANLEY CUP

Hockey fans were excited about Alexander Ovechkin playing in the NHL, but it didn't compare to the hype surrounding Sidney Crosby's professional debut. He was the young hotshot kid out of Nova Scotia and one of the leaders of the Canadian Junior Team. Every team wanted him, but the Pittsburgh Penguins were the only ones who got to have him. They chose Sidney with their first-round draft pick.

The Penguins seemed like a natural fit for Crosby. Evgeni Malkin, a young Russian superstar, was there to help Sidney with goal scoring. There were even a few friendly faces in the locker room: Sidney had played against Penguins' forward Maxime Talbot in the QMJHL and with goaltender Marc-André Fleury at the Junior Championships in 2004. The Penguins had already won two Stanley Cups in the early '90s, thanks to their superstar, Mario Lemieux, and they were ready for more. All the pieces fit perfectly: The team was young, the city of Pittsburgh loved hockey, and Sidney was the "chosen one" who would bring the Stanley Cup back to Pittsburgh.

With all that pressure to perform, Crosby could have stumbled early in his career. But Lemieux, who was now the Penguins' owner, was there to help. He told Crosby to keep a level head despite all of the press, and even invited Crosby to live with him and his family in the Pittsburgh suburb of Shadyside. Crosby even babysat Lemieux's kids and taught them some hockey moves!

Sidney's rookie season was great for him, but not for the Penguins. That season, Sidney wound up scoring 102 points, second among all rookies behind Alex Ovechkin, but the Penguins still finished last in the Atlantic Division. Everybody seemed excited, though, thanks in large part to Crosby's playing. He had more points that season than any Penguin since the famous Jaromir Jagr. He even won the Calder Trophy as the rookie of the year.

The 2006–2007 season was a lot different for the Penguins. Crosby scored 120 points— the most in the league—and finally led the Penguins to

Sidney poses with Mario Lemieux.

the play-offs, where they lost in the first round to the Ottawa Senators, the eventual Eastern Conference champions. Crosby also became the face of the NHL and appeared on TV ads and in commercials. Everywhere he went, he got mobbed by fans who wanted an autograph or reporters who wanted an interview with "Sid the Kid." He was even named captain—a leader, on and off the ice, who talks to refs and leads practices—making him the youngest team captain in NHL history.

Many people expected the 2007–2008 Pittsburgh Penguins to do even better, thanks to Crosby's ever-improving skills. And for a while, it looked like they would. Despite going on a losing streak in the middle of the season when Crosby sat injured with a high ankle sprain, Sidney came back and led the Penguins to the

Stanley Cup, beating the Ottawa Senators, New York Rangers, and Philadelphia Flyers along the way! But with his injury still nagging, Crosby and the Penguins couldn't overcome the Detroit Red Wings in the finals. The Penguins lost in six games, with the final game in Pittsburgh.

Crosby was shocked by the defeat. He even appeared in a commercial for the NHL where he vowed never to be beaten like that again.

And it looked like Crosby really meant it. Sidney came into the 2008–2009 season looking stronger than he ever had before. Despite a slump in the middle of the season, Crosby scored 103 points, took the Penguins to second place in the Atlantic Division, and all the way to the Stanley Cup Finals! He even managed to beat the Capitals and Alexander Ovechkin in the second round of the play-offs.

But in the finals, the Penguins found themselves facing the Detroit Red Wings once again. Detroit had just defeated Patrick Kane and the Blackhawks in the Western Conference Final. They were hungry for a championship, and many hockey fans thought Detroit could pull it off again.

Crosby was going to do everything he could to help his team win, though. In 24 games of the play-offs, he scored a total of 31 points, second only behind teammate Evgeni Malkin, who had 36. In the finals, the Penguins lost the first two games in Detroit, but then won the next two at home, thanks to three points and tremendous playing from Crosby. The teams split the next two games to force a showdown in Detroit with the Stanley Cup on the line.

In the middle of this important game, Crosby took a hard hit from Detroit's Johan Franzen. Crosby's knee was hurt, and he would have to sit out the rest of the game. He could only watch as his teammates

It's a Crosby-Ovechkin matchup!

struggled against the Red Wings.

His efforts throughout the year had been inspirational, though. Sidney's teammates refused to let their captain down. Max Talbot managed to score first, just a little over one minute into the second period. Almost nine minutes later, Talbot scored again off of a pass from teammate Chris Kunitz. But Detroit got a goal from Jonathan Ericsson just three minutes later. Winning wasn't going to be easy.

With the score 2–1 in favor of the

Crosby sustains an injury during the Stanley Cup Final.

Penguins, the team needed to hold on for just 27 more minutes of hockey. Crosby sat on the bench as the Red Wings attacked again and again. But Marc-André Fleury, the Penguins' goalie, was nearly perfect. He stopped shot after shot, including what seemed like the tying goal with just seconds left. Nicklas Lidstrom from Detroit had a wide-open net, but Fleury dived across to make the save and win the game!

The final buzzer went off, and Crosby couldn't believe it. The impossible had happened. The Penguins had won the game 2–1 and captured the Stanley Cup!

During the awards ceremony, Crosby finally got the chance to lift the Stanley Cup. At 34.5 pounds, the trophy definitely isn't light, but it must have seemed weightless in Crosby's grasp. This was what he'd been working for his entire life. He had led the

Penguins to hockey's ultimate prize. With a wicked slap shot and one Stanley Cup already under his belt, it's a good bet that he'll be on top again.

Crosby hoists the Stanley Cup!

OLYMPIC DREAMS

The 2010 Winter Olympics in Vancouver were one of the best Olympics yet, thanks in part to the exciting hockey tournament that closed the games. With 12 strong teams competing, any team could have made it to the gold medal round.

The tournament had many highs and lows. Alexander Ovechkin and Team Russia were bounced out by Team Canada in the quarterfinals by a score of 7–3. Jonathan Quick had to watch from the stands as fellow American goalie Ryan Miller's astonishing goaltending made him the MVP of the tournament. Even Sidney Crosby and Team Canada had a setback in the first round, losing to Team USA 5–3.

But that loss wasn't the end for the

Canadians. The first round of games was just to seed—or rank—teams for the final tournament, where every team would have a shot at the gold medal. One loss in the final round, however, would mean the end of any hope for Olympic glory. Because the Americans had won every game, they were highly "seeded" and got to face a lower-ranking team. Because of their first round loss, the Canadians would have to face tougher opponents.

But the thought of getting revenge on the US kept the Canadians alive. First they beat Germany, then Russia, and then Slovakia, for a spot in the gold medal game. Meanwhile, Team USA had put together one of their best Olympic runs ever. After taking the top spot in their division, Patrick Kane helped the US defeat the strong Swiss and Finnish teams with two goals. By doing that, the US once again had to face off against the Canadians, this time with the gold medal on the line!

The gold medal game started out badly for the Americans. Jonathan Toews of Canada scored first. This was the first time that the US had trailed in the 2010 Olympics! Then, Canadian Corey Perry got past Ryan Miller to make it 2–0.

But Patrick Kane wouldn't go down without a fight. With hard checks and blazing speed, he dished a pass in the second period to Ryan Kesler for the first American goal. Then, down by one with only 24 seconds left in the game, Kane shot the puck at the Canadian's net, where Zach Parise picked up the puck and scored to tie Team USA and Canada 2–2!

It all came down to sudden-death overtime, meaning the first team to score would win the game. The gold medal would come down to a single goal and everyone wondered, who would become a hero?

For seven minutes, Team USA and Team Canada fought back and forth, but neither side could get a goal. How long could this game go on?

But then, almost eight minutes into overtime, Sidney Crosby took a chance. Taking four Americans on while skating toward goalie Ryan Miller, he got Team Canada into position to score. Superstar teammate Jarome Iginla passed to Crosby

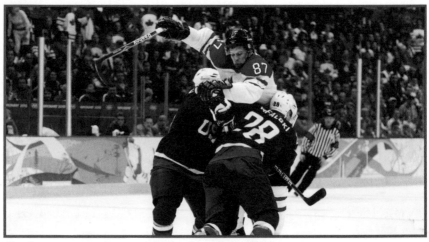

Crosby goes up against two players from Team USA.

from the boards. Sidney snapped the puck low and—amazingly—it got past Ryan Miller! The game was over: Canada 3, United States 2. Patrick Kane and the Americans had done their best, but Sidney Crosby had led the Canadians to another gold medal.

Kane, Quick, and Ovechkin were disappointed, and so were all the Russian and American fans. But there could only be one gold-medal winner, and Sidney Crosby and the Canadians were it. Lucky for these young stars, they will have another chance at hockey glory at the 2014 Winter Olympics in Sochi, Russia. Until then, Kane, Quick, Ovechkin, Crosby, and all the other young hotshots of hockey will just have to score goals, skate fast, and dream big while thrilling fans in the NHL.

Team Canada waves their flag in victory.